Family Tree

Organizer Book

Free Family Tree and Genealogy Templates

http://eepurl.com/hTrJqj

Thank you for supporting my small publishing business.
If you enjoy my books please consider leaving a review.
Cynthia Craig
Genealogy Hunter Press

The Ancestry Of

This family history record was compiled by:

_____

Started on:

_____

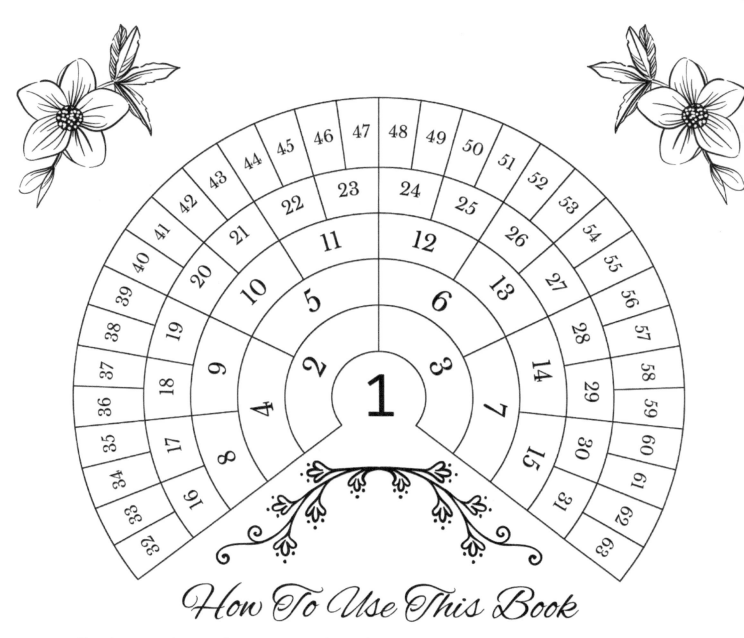

How To Use This Book

Each numbered space in the chart represents a direct ancestor. The following pages are numbered to match the chart. The 1st generation, space #1 is a single person or group of siblings that are the focus of the family tree.

#2 and #3 are the 2nd generation, parents of #1. #4 through #7, the 3rd generation, grandparents of #1. #8 through #15 the 4th generation, great grandparents of #1, and so on.

Traditionally, the even numbers represent male ancestors and the odd numbers are the female ancestors however, use the chart in the way that makes the most sense for your own family.

How to Use the Note Pages

A *Family Tree* or *Family Ancestry Record* can be so much more than a list of names, dates, and places. Use the *Note* pages to add additional details for each of your ancestors. Use these pages to make this book your own personalized detailed *Family History*.

Some Ideas For Your Note Pages

Hobbies
Family Recipes
Heirlooms
Immigration Information
Family Traditions
Pets
Automobiles
Occupations
Education
Awards
Extended Family

I think you get the idea. Have fun and create a beautiful family heirloom.

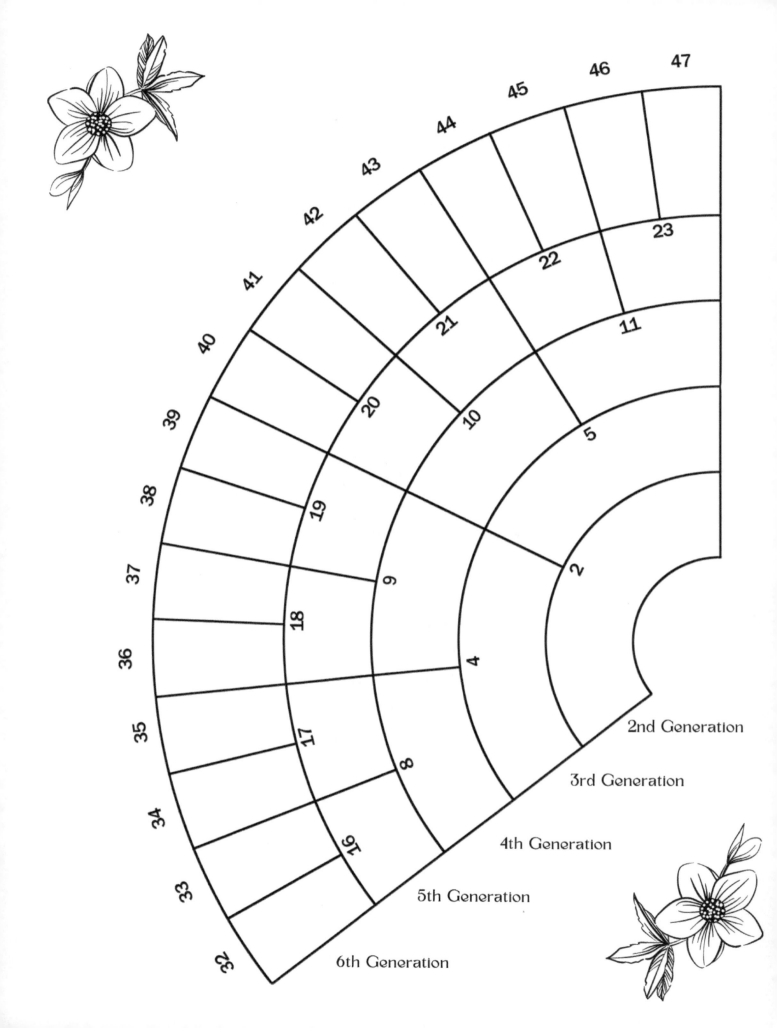

47
46
45
44
43
42
41
40
39
38
37
36
35
34
33
32

23
22
21
20
19
18
17
16

11
10
9
8

5
4

2

2nd Generation

3rd Generation

4th Generation

5th Generation

6th Generation

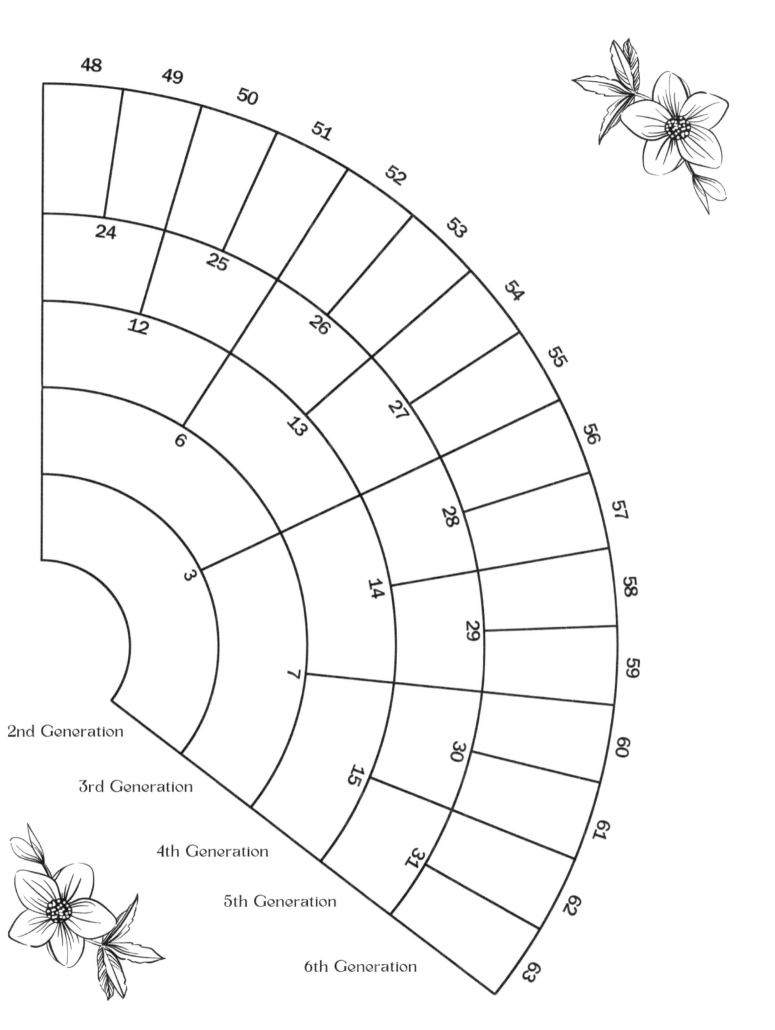

48

49

50

51

52

53

54

55

56

57

58

59

60

61

62

63

24

25

26

27

28

29

30

31

12

13

14

15

6

7

3

2nd Generation

3rd Generation

4th Generation

5th Generation

6th Generation

1

Name: ....

Birth Date: ....

Birth Place: ....

God Parents: ....

Nationality: .... **Religion:** ....

Education: .... **Occupation:** ....

Date of Death: .... **Cause of Death:** ....

Siblings: ....

....

....

Notes: ....

....

....

 *First Generation*

Notes

2

Name:

Birth Date: _____

Birth Place: _____

Godparents: _____

Nationality: _____ *Religion:* _____

Education: _____ *Occupation:* _____

Address: _____

_____

Date of Death: _____ *Cause of Death* _____

Siblings: _____

_____

_____

Marriages

Wife's Maiden Name: _____

Date: _____ *Place:* _____

Best Man: _____ *Maid of Honor:* _____

Groomsmen: _____

Bridesmaids: _____

Children

_____

_____

Second Generation

Notes

_____

_____

_____

_____

_____

_____

_____

_____

_____

_____

_____

_____

_____

_____

_____

_____

_____

_____

_____

_____

_____

3

Name:

Birth Date: _____

Birth Place: _____

Godparents: _____

Nationality: _____ *Religion:* _____

Education: _____ *Occupation:* _____

Address: _____

_____

Date of Death: _____ *Cause of Death* _____

Siblings: _____

_____

_____

Marriages

Wife's Maiden Name: _____

Date: _____ *Place:* _____

Best Man: _____ *Maid of Honor:* _____

Groomsmen: _____

Bridesmaids: _____

Children

_____

_____

Notes

4

Name:

Birth Date: _____

Birth Place: _____

Godparents: _____

Nationality: _____ *Religion:* _____

Education: _____ *Occupation:* _____

Address: _____

_____

Date of Death: _____ *Cause of Death* _____

Siblings: _____

_____

_____

Marriages

Wife's Maiden Name: _____

Date: _____ *Place:* _____

Best Man: _____ *Maid of Honor:* _____

Groomsmen: _____

Bridesmaids: _____

Children

_____

_____

Third Generation

Notes

5

Name:

Birth Date: _____

Birth Place: _____

Godparents: _____

Nationality: _____ *Religion:* _____

Education: _____ *Occupation:* _____

Address: _____

_____

Date of Death: _____ *Cause of Death* _____

Siblings: _____

_____

_____

Marriages

Wife's Maiden Name: _____

Date: _____ *Place:* _____

Best Man: _____ *Maid of Honor:* _____

Groomsmen: _____

Bridesmaids: _____

Children

_____

_____

Notes

6

Name:

Birth Date: _____

Birth Place: _____

Godparents: _____

Nationality: _____ **Religion:** _____

Education: _____ **Occupation:** _____

Address: _____

_____

Date of Death: _____ **Cause of Death** _____

Siblings: _____

_____

_____

Marriages

Wife's Maiden Name: _____

Date: _____ **Place:** _____

Best Man: _____ **Maid of Honor:** _____

Groomsmen: _____

Bridesmaids: _____

Children

_____

_____

Third Generation

Notes

_____

_____

_____

_____

_____

_____

_____

_____

_____

_____

_____

_____

_____

_____

_____

_____

_____

_____

_____

_____

_____

_____

7

Name:

Birth Date: _____

Birth Place: _____

Godparents: _____

Nationality: _____ *Religion:* _____

Education: _____ *Occupation:* _____

Address: _____

_____

Date of Death: _____ *Cause of Death* _____

Siblings: _____

_____

_____

Marriages

Wife's Maiden Name: _____

Date: _____ *Place:* _____

Best Man: _____ *Maid of Honor:* _____

Groomsmen: _____

Bridesmaids: _____

Children

_____

_____

Third Generation

Notes

8

Name:

Birth Date: _____

Birth Place: _____

Godparents: _____

Nationality: _____ *Religion:* _____

Education: _____ *Occupation:* _____

Address: _____

_____

Date of Death: _____ *Cause of Death* _____

Siblings: _____

_____

_____

Marriages

Wife's Maiden Name: _____

Date: _____ *Place:* _____

Best Man: _____ *Maid of Honor:* _____

Groomsmen: _____

Bridesmaids: _____

Children

_____

_____

Notes

9

Name:

Birth Date: _____

Birth Place: _____

Godparents: _____

Nationality: _____ *Religion:* _____

Education: _____ *Occupation:* _____

Address: _____

_____

Date of Death: _____ *Cause of Death* _____

Siblings: _____

_____

_____

Marriages

Wife's Maiden Name: _____

Date: _____ *Place:* _____

Best Man: _____ *Maid of Honor:* _____

Groomsmen: _____

Bridesmaids: _____

Children

_____

_____

Notes

10

Name:

Birth Date: _____

Birth Place: _____

Godparents: _____

Nationality: _____ *Religion:* _____

Education: _____ *Occupation:* _____

Address: _____

_____

Date of Death: _____ *Cause of Death* _____

Siblings: _____

_____

_____

Marriages

Wife's Maiden Name: _____

Date: _____ *Place:* _____

Best Man: _____ *Maid of Honor:* _____

Groomsmen: _____

Bridesmaids: _____

Children

_____

_____

Fourth Generation

Notes

11

Name:

Birth Date: _____

Birth Place: _____

Godparents: _____

Nationality: _____ *Religion:* _____

Education: _____ *Occupation:* _____

Address: _____

_____

Date of Death: _____ *Cause of Death* _____

Siblings: _____

_____

_____

Marriages

Wife's Maiden Name: _____

Date: _____ *Place:* _____

Best Man: _____ *Maid of Honor:* _____

Groomsmen: _____

Bridesmaids: _____

Children

_____

_____

Fourth Generation

Notes

12

Name: _____

Birth Date: _____

Birth Place: _____

Godparents: _____

Nationality: _____ Religion: _____

Education: _____ Occupation: _____

Address: _____

_____

Date of Death: _____ Cause of Death _____

Siblings: _____

_____

_____

Marriages

Wife's Maiden Name: _____

Date: _____ Place: _____

Best Man: _____ Maid of Honor: _____

Groomsmen: _____

Bridesmaids: _____

Children

_____

_____

Notes

13

Name:

Birth Date: _____

Birth Place: _____

Godparents: _____

Nationality: _____ Religion: _____

Education: _____ Occupation: _____

Address: _____

_____

Date of Death: _____ Cause of Death _____

Siblings: _____

_____

_____

Marriages

Wife's Maiden Name: _____

Date: _____ Place: _____

Best Man: _____ Maid of Honor: _____

Groomsmen: _____

Bridesmaids: _____

Children

_____

_____

Notes

14

Name: _____

Birth Date: _____

Birth Place: _____

Godparents: _____

Nationality: _____ **Religion:** _____

Education: _____ **Occupation:** _____

Address: _____

_____

Date of Death: _____ **Cause of Death** _____

Siblings: _____

_____

_____

Marriages

Wife's Maiden Name: _____

Date: _____ **Place:** _____

Best Man: _____ **Maid of Honor:** _____

Groomsmen: _____

Bridesmaids: _____

Children

_____

_____

Notes

_____
_____
_____
_____
_____
_____
_____
_____
_____
_____
_____
_____
_____
_____
_____
_____
_____
_____
_____
_____
_____

15

Name:

Birth Date: _____

Birth Place: _____

Godparents: _____

Nationality: _____ *Religion:* _____

Education: _____ *Occupation:* _____

Address: _____

_____

Date of Death: _____ *Cause of Death* _____

Siblings: _____

_____

_____

Marriages

Wife's Maiden Name: _____

Date: _____ *Place:* _____

Best Man: _____ *Maid of Honor:* _____

Groomsmen: _____

Bridesmaids: _____

Children

_____

_____

Notes

_____
_____
_____
_____
_____
_____
_____
_____
_____
_____
_____
_____
_____
_____
_____
_____
_____
_____
_____
_____
_____
_____

16

Name: _____

Birth Date: _____

Birth Place: _____

Nationality: _____ *Religion:* _____

Education: _____ *Occupation:* _____

Date of Death: _____ *Cause of Death* _____

Siblings: _____

_____

17

Name: _____

Birth Date: _____

Birth Place: _____

Nationality: _____ *Religion:* _____

Education: _____ *Occupation:* _____

Date of Death: _____ *Cause of Death* _____

Siblings: _____

_____

Children: _____

_____

_____

Notes

18

Name:

Birth Date: _____

Birth Place: _____

Nationality: _____ *Religion:* _____

Education: _____ *Occupation:* _____

Date of Death: _____ *Cause of Death* _____

Siblings: _____

_____

19

Name:

Birth Date: _____

Birth Place: _____

Nationality: _____ *Religion:* _____

Education: _____ *Occupation:* _____

Date of Death: _____ *Cause of Death* _____

Siblings: _____

_____

Children: _____

_____

_____

Notes

_____
_____
_____
_____
_____
_____
_____
_____
_____
_____
_____
_____
_____
_____
_____
_____
_____
_____
_____
_____
_____
_____

20 Name: _____

Birth Date: _____

Birth Place: _____

Nationality: _____ Religion: _____

Education: _____ Occupation: _____

Date of Death: _____ Cause of Death _____

Siblings: _____

_____

21 Name: _____

Birth Date: _____

Birth Place: _____

Nationality: _____ Religion: _____

Education: _____ Occupation: _____

Date of Death: _____ Cause of Death _____

Siblings: _____

_____

Children: _____

_____

_____

Notes

22

Name:

Birth Date: _____

Birth Place: _____

Nationality: _____ *Religion:* _____

Education: _____ *Occupation:* _____

Date of Death: _____ *Cause of Death* _____

Siblings: _____

_____

23

Name:

Birth Date: _____

Birth Place: _____

Nationality: _____ *Religion:* _____

Education: _____ *Occupation:* _____

Date of Death: _____ *Cause of Death* _____

Siblings: _____

_____

Children: _____

_____

_____

Fifth Generation

Notes

_____
_____
_____
_____
_____
_____
_____
_____
_____
_____
_____
_____
_____
_____
_____
_____
_____
_____
_____
_____
_____
_____
_____

24

Name:

Birth Date: _____

Birth Place: _____

Nationality: _____ Religion: _____

Education: _____ Occupation: _____

Date of Death: _____ Cause of Death _____

Siblings: _____

_____

25

Name:

Birth Date: _____

Birth Place: _____

Nationality: _____ Religion: _____

Education: _____ Occupation: _____

Date of Death: _____ Cause of Death _____

Siblings: _____

_____

Children: _____

_____

_____

Notes

_____
_____
_____
_____
_____
_____
_____
_____
_____
_____
_____
_____
_____
_____
_____
_____
_____
_____
_____
_____
_____
_____
_____
_____

26

Name:

Birth Date: _____

Birth Place: _____

Nationality: _____ Religion: _____

Education: _____ Occupation: _____

Date of Death: _____ Cause of Death _____

Siblings: _____

_____

27

Name:

Birth Date: _____

Birth Place: _____

Nationality: _____ Religion: _____

Education: _____ Occupation: _____

Date of Death: _____ Cause of Death _____

Siblings: _____

_____

Children: _____

_____

_____

Fifth Generation

Notes

28

Name: _____

Birth Date: _____

Birth Place: _____

Nationality: _____   Religion: _____

Education: _____   Occupation: _____

Date of Death: _____   Cause of Death _____

Siblings: _____

_____

29

Name: _____

Birth Date: _____

Birth Place: _____

Nationality: _____   Religion: _____

Education: _____   Occupation: _____

Date of Death: _____   Cause of Death _____

Siblings: _____

_____

Children: _____

_____

_____

Notes

30

Name:

Birth Date: _____

Birth Place: _____

Nationality: _____ Religion: _____

Education: _____ Occupation: _____

Date of Death: _____ Cause of Death _____

Siblings: _____

_____

31

Name:

Birth Date: _____

Birth Place: _____

Nationality: _____ Religion: _____

Education: _____ Occupation: _____

Date of Death: _____ Cause of Death _____

Siblings: _____

_____

Children: _____

_____

_____

Notes

32

Name:

Birth Date: _____

Birth Place: _____

Nationality: _____ Religion: _____

Education: _____ Occupation: _____

Date of Death: _____ Cause of Death _____

Siblings: _____

_____

33

Name:

Birth Date: _____

Birth Place: _____

Nationality: _____ Religion: _____

Education: _____ Occupation: _____

Date of Death: _____ Cause of Death _____

Siblings: _____

_____

Children: _____

_____

_____

Notes

_____
_____
_____
_____
_____
_____
_____
_____
_____
_____
_____
_____
_____
_____
_____
_____
_____
_____
_____
_____
_____
_____
_____

34

Name:

Birth Date: _____

Birth Place: _____

Nationality: _____ *Religion:* _____

Education: _____ *Occupation:* _____

Date of Death: _____ *Cause of Death* _____

Siblings: _____

_____

35

Name:

Birth Date: _____

Birth Place: _____

Nationality: _____ *Religion:* _____

Education: _____ *Occupation:* _____

Date of Death: _____ *Cause of Death* _____

Siblings: _____

_____

Children: _____

_____

_____

Notes

36

Name:

Birth Date: _____

Birth Place: _____

Nationality: _____ Religion: _____

Education: _____ Occupation: _____

Date of Death: _____ Cause of Death _____

Siblings: _____

_____

37

Name:

Birth Date: _____

Birth Place: _____

Nationality: _____ Religion: _____

Education: _____ Occupation: _____

Date of Death: _____ Cause of Death _____

Siblings: _____

_____

Children: _____

_____

_____

Notes

38

Name:

Birth Date: _____

Birth Place: _____

Nationality: _____ *Religion:* _____

Education: _____ *Occupation:* _____

Date of Death: _____ *Cause of Death* _____

Siblings: _____

_____

39

Name:

Birth Date: _____

Birth Place: _____

Nationality: _____ *Religion:* _____

Education: _____ *Occupation:* _____

Date of Death: _____ *Cause of Death* _____

Siblings: _____

_____

Children: _____

_____

_____

Notes

40

Name:

Birth Date: _____

Birth Place: _____

Nationality: _____ Religion: _____

Education: _____ Occupation: _____

Date of Death: _____ Cause of Death _____

Siblings: _____

_____

41

Name:

Birth Date: _____

Birth Place: _____

Nationality: _____ Religion: _____

Education: _____ Occupation: _____

Date of Death: _____ Cause of Death _____

Siblings: _____

_____

Children: _____

_____

_____

Notes

42

Name:

Birth Date: _____

Birth Place: _____

Nationality: _____ Religion: _____

Education: _____ Occupation: _____

Date of Death: _____ Cause of Death _____

Siblings: _____

_____

43

Name:

Birth Date: _____

Birth Place: _____

Nationality: _____ Religion: _____

Education: _____ Occupation: _____

Date of Death: _____ Cause of Death _____

Siblings: _____

_____

Children: _____

_____

_____

Notes

44

Name:

Birth Date: _____

Birth Place: _____

Nationality: _____ Religion: _____

Education: _____ Occupation: _____

Date of Death: _____ Cause of Death _____

Siblings: _____

_____

45

Name:

Birth Date: _____

Birth Place: _____

Nationality: _____ Religion: _____

Education: _____ Occupation: _____

Date of Death: _____ Cause of Death _____

Siblings: _____

_____

Children: _____

_____

_____

Notes

46

Name:

Birth Date: _____

Birth Place: _____

Nationality: _____   *Religion*: _____

Education: _____   *Occupation*: _____

Date of Death: _____   *Cause of Death* _____

Siblings: _____

_____

47

Name:

Birth Date: _____

Birth Place: _____

Nationality: _____   *Religion*: _____

Education: _____   *Occupation*: _____

Date of Death: _____   *Cause of Death* _____

Siblings: _____

_____

Children: _____

_____

_____

Notes

48

Name: _____

Birth Date: _____

Birth Place: _____

Nationality: _____ Religion: _____

Education: _____ Occupation: _____

Date of Death: _____ Cause of Death _____

Siblings: _____

_____

49

Name: _____

Birth Date: _____

Birth Place: _____

Nationality: _____ Religion: _____

Education: _____ Occupation: _____

Date of Death: _____ Cause of Death _____

Siblings: _____

_____

Children: _____

_____

_____

Notes

50

Name:

Birth Date: _____

Birth Place: _____

Nationality: _____ *Religion:* _____

Education: _____ *Occupation:* _____

Date of Death: _____ *Cause of Death* _____

Siblings: _____

_____

51

Name:

Birth Date: _____

Birth Place: _____

Nationality: _____ *Religion:* _____

Education: _____ *Occupation:* _____

Date of Death: _____ *Cause of Death* _____

Siblings: _____

_____

Children: _____

_____

_____

Notes

52

Name:

Birth Date: _____

Birth Place: _____

Nationality: _____ *Religion:* _____

Education: _____ *Occupation:* _____

Date of Death: _____ *Cause of Death* _____

Siblings: _____

_____

53

Name:

Birth Date: _____

Birth Place: _____

Nationality: _____ *Religion:* _____

Education: _____ *Occupation:* _____

Date of Death: _____ *Cause of Death* _____

Siblings: _____

_____

Children: _____

_____

_____

Notes

54

Name:

Birth Date: _____

Birth Place: _____

Nationality: _____ *Religion:* _____

Education: _____ *Occupation:* _____

Date of Death: _____ *Cause of Death* _____

Siblings: _____

_____

55

Name:

Birth Date: _____

Birth Place: _____

Nationality: _____ *Religion:* _____

Education: _____ *Occupation:* _____

Date of Death: _____ *Cause of Death* _____

Siblings: _____

_____

Children: _____

_____

_____

Notes

_____

_____

_____

_____

_____

_____

_____

_____

_____

_____

_____

_____

_____

_____

_____

_____

_____

_____

_____

_____

_____

_____

56

Name: _____

Birth Date: _____

Birth Place: _____

Nationality: _____ *Religion:* _____

Education: _____ *Occupation:* _____

Date of Death: _____ *Cause of Death* _____

Siblings: _____

_____

57

Name: _____

Birth Date: _____

Birth Place: _____

Nationality: _____ *Religion:* _____

Education: _____ *Occupation:* _____

Date of Death: _____ *Cause of Death* _____

Siblings: _____

_____

Children: _____

_____

_____

Notes

58

Name:

Birth Date: _____

Birth Place: _____

Nationality: _____ Religion: _____

Education: _____ Occupation: _____

Date of Death: _____ Cause of Death _____

Siblings: _____

_____

59

Name:

Birth Date: _____

Birth Place: _____

Nationality: _____ Religion: _____

Education: _____ Occupation: _____

Date of Death: _____ Cause of Death _____

Siblings: _____

_____

Children: _____

_____

_____

Notes

60

Name: _____

Birth Date: _____

Birth Place: _____

Nationality: _____ Religion: _____

Education: _____ Occupation: _____

Date of Death: _____ Cause of Death _____

Siblings: _____

_____

61

Name: _____

Birth Date: _____

Birth Place: _____

Nationality: _____ Religion: _____

Education: _____ Occupation: _____

Date of Death: _____ Cause of Death _____

Siblings: _____

_____

Children: _____

_____

_____

Sixth Generation

Notes

62

Name:

Birth Date: _____

Birth Place: _____

Nationality: _____ *Religion:* _____

Education: _____ *Occupation:* _____

Date of Death: _____ *Cause of Death* _____

Siblings: _____

_____

63

Name:

Birth Date: _____

Birth Place: _____

Nationality: _____ *Religion:* _____

Education: _____ *Occupation:* _____

Date of Death: _____ *Cause of Death* _____

Siblings: _____

_____

Children: _____

_____

_____

Notes

 # Notes

Notes

Notes

Notes

Military Service

Name _____

Service _____

Rank _____

Dates _____

Notes _____

_____

_____

_____

Name _____

Service _____

Rank _____

Dates _____

Notes _____

_____

_____

_____

Name _____

Service _____

Rank _____

Dates _____

Notes _____

_____

_____

_____

Military Service

Name

Service

Rank

Dates

Notes

Name

Service

Rank

Dates

Notes

Name

Service

Rank

Dates

Notes

Military Service

Name _____

Service _____

Rank _____

Dates _____

Notes _____

_____

_____

_____

Name _____

Service _____

Rank _____

Dates _____

Notes _____

_____

_____

_____

Name _____

Service _____

Rank _____

Dates _____

Notes _____

_____

_____

_____

Military Service

Name

Service

Rank

Dates

Notes

Name

Service

Rank

Dates

Notes

Name

Service

Rank

Dates

Notes

Notes

Notes

Research Checklist

Names	Birth Record	Marriage Record	Death Certificate	Obituary	Burial Records	School Records

Property Records	Religious Records	Military Records	Health Records	Immigration Records	Adoption Records	Paddports

Research Checklist

Names	Birth Record	Marriage Record	Death Certificate	Obituary	Burial Records	School Records

Property Records

Religious Records

Military Records

Health Records

Immigration Records

Adoption Records

Paddports

Research Checklist

Names	Birth Record	Marriage Record	Death Certificate	Obituary	Burial Records	School Records

Property Records	Religious Records	Military Records	Health Records	Immigration Records	Adoption Records	Paddports

Sources of Information

Date	Description of Source	Location of Source	Notes

Sources of Information

Date	Description of Source	Location of Source	Notes

Sources of Information

Date	Description of Source	Location of Source	Notes

Sources of Information

Date	Description of Source	Location of Source	Notes

Helpful Resources

National Archives

https://www.archives.gov

Family Search

https://www.familysearch.org/en/

United States Census Bureau

https://www.census.gov/topics/population/genealogy.html

USGenWeb Project

http://www.usgenweb.org/

Access Genealogy

https://accessgenealogy.com/

Legacy.com

https://www.legacy.com/obituaries/local

Cyndi's List

https://www.cyndislist.com/

Rootsweb

https://home.rootsweb.com/

Society of American Archivists

https://www2.archivists.org/usingarchives

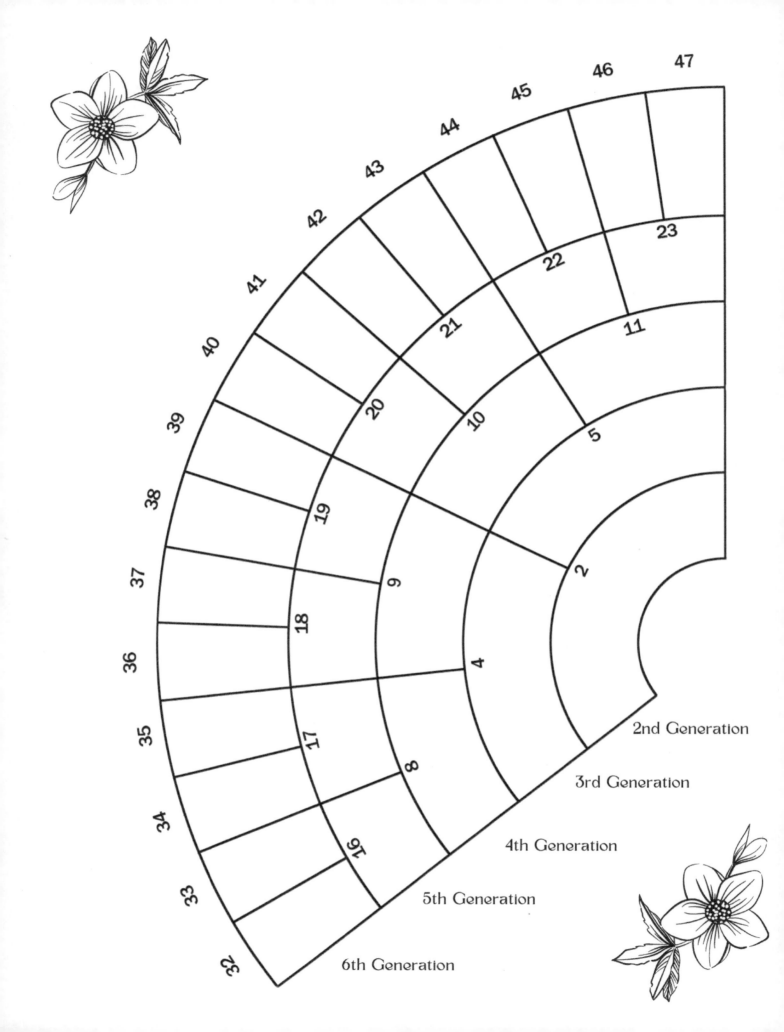

32
33
34
35
36
37
38
39
40
41
42
43
44
45
46
47

23
22
21
20
19
18
17
16

11
10
9
8

5
4

2

2nd Generation

3rd Generation

4th Generation

5th Generation

6th Generation

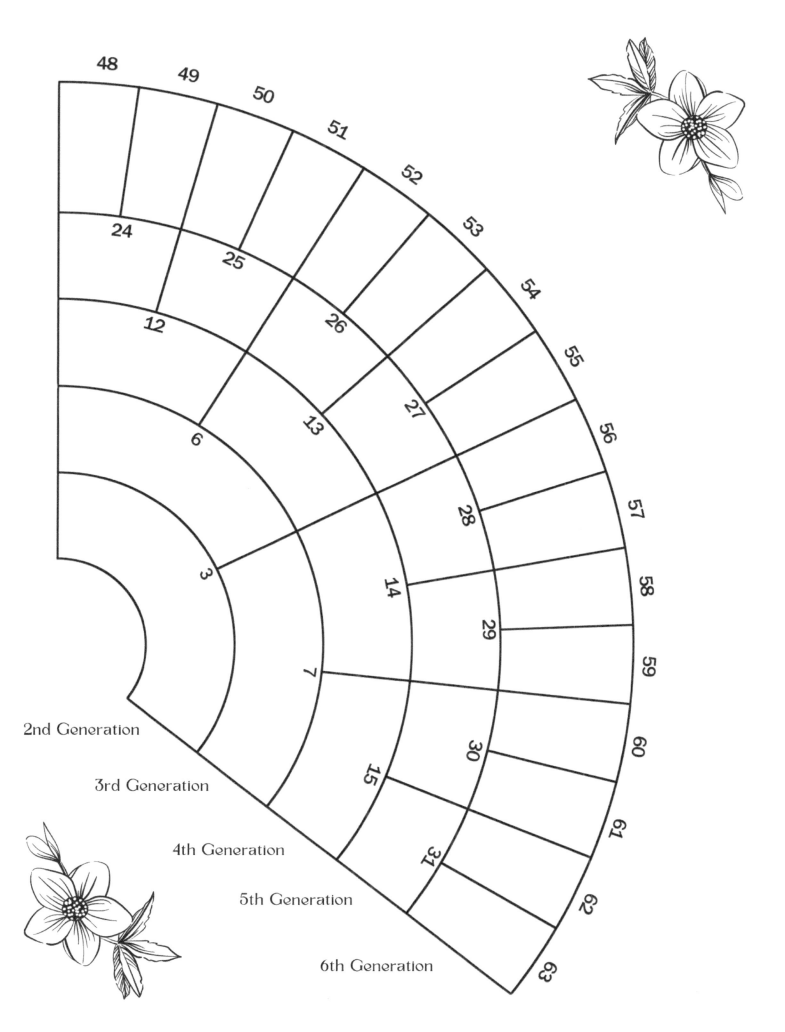

48

49

50

51

52

53

54

55

56

57

58

59

60

61

62

63

24

25

26

27

28

29

30

31

12

13

14

15

6

7

3

2nd Generation

3rd Generation

4th Generation

5th Generation

6th Generation

Free Family Tree and Genealogy Templates

http://eepurl.com/hTrJqj

Thank you for supporting my small publishing business.
If you enjoy my books please consider leaving a review.
Cynthia Craig
Genealogy Hunter Press

Printed in France by Amazon
Brétigny-sur-Orge, FR

20632242R00065